Table of contents

THERE'S NO PLACE LIKE HOME

Life on our planet can be found in every nook and cranny. The place inhabited by a particular animal species is called a habitat. This is the same place where said animals look for shelter or food, start a family, or raise their offspring. It's also true that local inhabitants are fantastically adapted to living at that particular spot. Can you imagine a polar bear living in a scorched desert? What would it have to do in order to survive there? Each animal dweller on Earth has an area where life is just the best.

FROM DESERT TO ICE LANDS

Inhabitants of the animal kingdom can be found at any place you can name: in deserts where it's extremely hot during the day and bitterly cold at night; in dark caves where you can't see a thing; in shallow waters and at the bottom of the ocean. Life can be observed at mountaintops and in freezing polar regions. So let's visit all of these places together and meet their inhabitants! ◂

DIFFERENT COUNTRIES HAVE DIFFERENT CUSTOMS

A habitat offers its inhabitants only what's **best and most characteristic** for them – be it plants, climate, or rocks. What grows and lives in a particular habitat directly determines the number and diversity of local inhabitants. On dry land, tropical rain forests where it's always warm and damp pride themselves on housing the largest number of animal species in the world. Under the surface of the oceans, however, most animal species can be found living near coral reefs. ▸

I'LL DEAL WITH THIS SOMEHOW

How come penguins are able to survive the freezing Antarctica winter? Do they put on a sweater? Does a camel carry a water bottle around the desert so that it can have a drink? Not at all. Be it cold, hot, dark, or light, all inhabitants of any particular territory **know how to manage**. ▲

WHAT LONG HAIRS YOU HAVE!

Nature made it so that animals are as **equipped to deal with their environment as possible**. Some are protected by shaggy fur or thick plumage, others by ingenious camouflage. There are also some clever fellows who can hide from unfavorable weather in a shelter they built themselves. Each species is different, but the reason for this is always the same: to adapt as much as possible, and thus make one's own life more pleasant. ►

WHAT USED TO BE IS NO MORE

Naturally, habitats gradually change over time, be it due to sudden incidents like earthquakes or because of permanent natural changes, such as erosion. Habitats aren't the only thing affected by these **changes**; so are their inhabitants–animals. Animals as we know them today are quite different from those that settled on dry land over 400 million years ago. ◄

DESERT

HOT, DRY REGION

Unbearable heat, scorching sun, and sand burning your feet. Where do you think we are? That's right, in the desert, one of the most hostile places on Earth. There's no water in sight and very few plants, and when the wind starts blowing, you can expect a blinding sandstorm to arrive. Who would live in such conditions? You'll probably be surprised to discover that quite a diverse mix of inhabitants would.

WHAT IS A DESERT?

Deserts are **infertile regions** with a dry climate, extreme temperatures, and **very little precipitation**. The sun beats down on the ground all day, making it really hot! Temperatures can be very hot during the day but drop below the freezing point at night. ▼

DANGERS OF DESERTS

The hostile environment isn't the only **danger** around the desert: it's joined by various predators or poisonous creatures waiting for a snack to come closer. Desert inhabitants need to be on their toes if they want to escape unharmed. Phew! ◀

Day and night in the desert

HOW TO SURVIVE IN THE DESERT?

How can animals survive in such harsh conditions? Easily–they adapted to the great temperature fluctuations, lack of water and food. Furthermore, even deserts have places where life thrives: the **green oases** where there's no shortage of moisture. ▼

ANIMALS AREN'T THE ONLY ONES WHO CAN ADAPT

People can cope with living in the desert too. However, they need a shelter to hide from the desert climate. Be it a permanent residence or portable home, it protects them from heat, cold, winds, and rain. Even clothing shields them–he who's thoroughly covered will make it big in the desert. ▼

I'LL MANAGE

How can you escape the scorching sun? Easily–just crawl underground or go outside only after dark when it's not so hot. Have you ever wondered why desert animals are **light in color**? It's because light skin doesn't absorb as much heat as dark skin does, and it additionally helps the animal to blend in with the surrounding sand. ▼

HE WHO ADAPTS WINS

Some animals have large ears which give off extra heat. Others boast a body or pair of feet adapted to moving in the sand. And there are even those who can do without water for a very long time. Some plants have unusually long roots that enable them to reach underground water, while others are able to keep liquid in for quite a while. ▲

DESERT INHABITANTS

HEAT ENTHUSIASTS

SANDGROUSE

Sandgrouse males can be compared to a sponge. That's because they have special frayed feathers on their belly which are capable of **absorbing water** just like a sponge! This allows them to absorb water from an oasis or watering place and carry it to their young, who then drink by sucking on the feathers. ▶

GERBIL

This little rodent dwells in an **underground den**, which is not only spacious but also beautifully cool. Because gerbils have brown-beige fur, they nicely blend in with their surroundings when they dare to go outside. They don't need to worry about insufficient amounts of water because they can turn their body fat into water! ▶

FENNEC

This shaggy little fox has **large ears** that function as **heat exchangers**, meaning they prevent overheating. The ears also serve as a revolving radar to help with hunting–they locate prey even if it's underground. Fennecs have furry paws which protect them from the hot sand, just like shoes. And as if that wasn't enough, these animals can do without water for a very long time. ▼

THORNY DRAGON

Are you wondering who these handsome guys are? Thorny dragons surely know how to put their thorns to good use. The thorns not only protect their owners from getting attacked but also **gather water** on the animal's back when it's raining. The water then flows through small ducts directly into the thorny dragon's mouth. ▲

HEAD-STANDER BEETLE – THE DESERT YOGI

Why does the beetle stand on its head? Did it get silly from the sweltering heat? No, it didn't–in fact, this is how it deals with the heat! The head-stander beetle spends the night buried in the sand, but when night fog arrives, it's outside in a flash and **starts gathering dew**. In order to gather as much of it as possible, it lifts its behind up in the air. The dew drops then flow right down into its mouth. What a smart little devil! ▶

Beetle gathering dew

SAHARA SAND VIPER

This snake spends the hottest part of each day **buried in the sand**. As it patiently waits for its prey, it can mask itself so well that only its eyes and nostrils are visible. At night, the viper leaves its shelter and moves on the sand by undulating sideways. This makes moving around easier and the sand doesn't burn so much! ▲

CAMEL – THE SHIP OF THE DESERT

It's well known that camels can do without water for a very long time. Contrary to popular belief, they store fat, not water in their humps, but at the same time, they can turn the stored fat into water and energy. They have long eyelashes, furry ears, and closable nostrils, all of which protect them from sand. Even their legs are properly adapted so that they don't sink into the fine sand. It seems like camels are perfectly adapted to living in the desert, wouldn't you say? ▶

The ship of the desert

MOUNTAINS

ROCK GIANTS

Mountains, or to be more precise, high mountains, are one of the highest and least accessible places on our planet. Living conditions in valleys are usually acceptable, but the higher we go, the fewer plants we find, and there may be only rocks, snow, and ice as far as the eye can see. Despite this, local animal inhabitants are well adapted to living in such conditions.

A MOUNTAIN HOME

Locals may be shy since they're not used to having company, but they deal with the mountain conditions as best as they can. How would you otherwise explain that you can encounter predators, birds, and insects up there? ◂

An avalanche

MOUNTAINS & HIGH MOUNTAINS

A full fifth of our planet is covered by huge mountain ranges. That's quite a lot, wouldn't you say? People rarely set foot there. Nobody can permanently live **at mountaintops**, which is why animals are mostly found at lower-lying places. But life is no walk in the park even there, and local dwellers should be viewed as pretty bold for that reason. ▾

Mountain landscape

DANGERS OF THE MOUNTAINS

Some mountains are miles above sea level. It's bitterly cold at the top. A great danger is posed by avalanches, or snow rapidly sliding down the mountainside. An avalanche can speed down a mountain and destroy anything it encounters. Other mountain ranges are covered in ice. ▴

I CAN GET AROUND

Protective coloration protects and masks animals in order to help them blend in with their surroundings as well as possible. This enables them to get a bit to eat. Some animals are able to move well even over steep areas. Their shaggy fur protects them from the cold. ▲

LIVING IN THE MOUNTAINS

Living **at the foot of steep mountains** requires the right climbing equipment: strong toes, paws, or hooves, and especially a lack of fear. No one who's prone to vertigo would survive there. Having shaggy fur and excellent eyesight greatly pays off. Anyone who can't survive at higher regions during the winter descends to lower places, returning only when the weather eases off. ▼

MOUNTAIN PEOPLE

People who are used to living at high altitudes have no issue with ascending high mountains. If others wish to look around the top of the highest mountains, they need to make proper preparations and allow their body to gradually get used to new altitudes, unless they're willing to suffer a possible tragedy. **Sherpas**, for example, help mountain expeditions, prepare trails, and set up camps. ▲

MOUNTAIN INHABITANTS

HEAD IN THE CLOUDS

SNOW LEOPARD

This rare animal is greatly equipped to withstand the mountains. It has convenient **spotty coloration** and can easily hide among the surrounding stones and snow. Wide furry paws protect a snow leopard from snow and prevent it from slipping on rocks. This excellent hunter can also jump very well due to its strong hind legs! ▸

GELADA

These relatives of baboons live at high places in Ethiopia and are quite the prodigious mountain climbers. At night, they sleep at rocky precipices in large herds, which keeps them safe from Ethiopian wolves. How smart! They're completely free from harm this way. ▴

WILD YAK

Yaks have no problem living in mountains, since they're protected from the cold by **long, shaggy fur**. But few people know that a yak's body is adapted to high altitudes so well that the animal is utterly unable to live at low-lying, warmer places. It would most definitely get sick there. Usually, yaks stay at an altitude high above the ground. They have a rather large heart and pair of lungs, which is why breathing is quite easy for them up there, at least when compared to us. ▴

LLAMA

Llamas live in the Andean Mountains where weather is the most changeable on the planet. Just blink and there's a fierce storm. It gets colder and starts snowing. Because llamas are equipped with a thick fur, such changes in temperatures have no chance to damage their calm. ◂

RED PANDA

Unlike other animals that sleep through the winter, red pandas can't afford such luxury. When winter arrives at the high places that red pandas inhabit, they instead look for food–**bamboo**–and avoid lower-laying regions where they would be unable to find it. A shaggy coat and pair of hairy paws protect them from the cold. ▼

Couple of red pandas

MOUNTAIN GOAT

Meet one of the best animal mountain climbers. They have special **hooves** with two toes that allow them to maintain balance without even thinking about it. A mountain goat's shaggy coat protects it from the cold and from sharp winds. And furthermore, the light color provides great camouflage in the snow! ▼

Skilled rock climber

BAR-HEADED GOOSE

These flying daredevils rank among the **birds that fly the highest**. They stay at alpine meadows over the course of summer but then leave to spend the winter at their wintering site. They need to cross the Himalayas on this route! They have a large wingspan and never cease to flap their wings during the flight. These super fliers have no problem dealing with the lack of oxygen at high altitudes. ▲

RAIN FOREST

GREEN VEGETATION TEEMING WITH LIFE

Hot weather, high humidity, and green vegetation everywhere the eye can see. That's a rain forest-a place where it's hot just like in the desert, but where rain is the rule, not the exception. Due to the sufficient moisture, rain forests host an incredible amount of plants and animals. How do they all live around here? Aren't they exposed to more danger than they would have been if they lived somewhere else? Let's set out for the rain forest and meet its inhabitants!

HE WHO HIDES WINS

It's great fun to play hide-and-seek among so many plants. But it's not really a game around here and more like trying not to end up as somebody's snack. Some animals rely on living in the treetops where they're out of reach of predators. Others depend on their protective coloring, which makes them nearly invisible. ▼

UP & BEYOND

Many rainforest inhabitants are able to live both **on the ground and in the treetops**. It needs to be said, though, that they're safer above the forest floor. That's because they're better equipped to live higher up: the animals have strong front legs which enable them to climb trees well. If they have a tail, it often functions as a "third hand" to hold onto branches. As you can see, they certainly don't lack useful tools... ▼

DANGERS OF THE JUNGLE

Jungles can be described as divided into several **layers**. The bottom one is damp and dim, with little sunshine. On the other hand, the treetops are simply bustling with life. People must be constantly on their toes, though; just about anything or anyone can hide in the thick growth... ▲

CONSPICUOUS, OR INCONSPICUOUS?

What do you think: is it better not to be seen or to draw attention to yourself? You can do both in the rain forest. Some animals are indistinguishable from leaves, twigs, or blossoms. Having a neutral green or brown coloration is also nothing to sneeze at. Others are amazingly colorful. But don't they attract needless attention? On the contrary, they're quite smart; either they're poisonous or imitate the coloration of actual poisonous species in order not to get eaten. ▼

Walking flower mantis

Poison dart frog

NATIVE PEOPLES

Rain forests host a lot of native tribes who still live in harmony with nature and have little to no knowledge of modern conveniences. The rain forest is their home, which is why they know it inside out. Men of the Yanomami tribe are considered the best hunters in the world because they can hear the slightest sounds and can strike the offending animal with pinpoint accuracy. ◄

WHAT IS A RAIN FOREST?

Even though rain forests cover only approximately 3% of our planet's surface, you can find a huge amount of different plants and animals in them. Why so? Because it rains each day in rain forests, there's a lot of sunshine, and the plants grow really fast and high. Rain forests are nicknamed **the lungs of the Earth** because such a large number of plants can produce a great amount of oxygen. Most of the local animals can be found up the in treetops. ►

RAIN FOREST INHABITANTS

LIVING UP IN THE TREETOPS

JAGUAR

Dots on a jaguar's body provide an excellent camouflage in rain forests. This big cat lives on the ground where little sunlight falls. The play of shadow and light is very advantageous for this hunter. It's no wonder that the jaguar is one of the largest predators in the entire jungle. It treads quietly on its paws and attacks quickly. Jaguars are even able to climb trees, which allows them to surprise their prey by leaping on it and attacking. ►

GEOFFROY'S SPIDER MONKEY

This animal is considered one of the most nimble tree-dwelling monkeys. It has **long fingers** whose function is similar to that of hooks–the monkey simply hangs on a branch and then moves from one branch to another by swinging. The long tail serves as a sort of "fifth" hand that allows the animal to better hold onto branches when climbing through the treetops. ▲

RED-EYED TREE FROG

This frog is one of the most multicolored amphibians on Earth. During the day, though, it uses **camouflage**: the frog remains calm and maintains an unchanging position, with limbs tucked under its body and red eyes closed. You'd never be able to distinguish it from leaves when it's like this. Red-eyed tree frogs have soft pads on their feet which enable them to attach themselves to leaves. These animals are great jumpers and climbers. ▼

BROWN-THROATED SLOTH

This smiling creature feels quite settled high up the treetops. A sloth's fingers have long curved claws that allow it to hang from branches like it's no big deal. These animals have an inconspicuous coloration, very often with a greenish tinge which is caused by the algae growing on their fur. Additionally, sloths are quiet and move slowly. This makes them the ideal, well-masked jungle dwellers. ◄

WALKING FLOWER MANTIS

Did you think that I have a pretty flower to show you? Not at all–this is an insect! A walking flower mantis is a mantis species that resembles an orchid blossom. This "**disguise**" is, no exaggeration, quite perfect–its legs even look like petals! Walking flower mantises use their looks to easily attract pollinators, such as bees and other insects, and turn them into their dinner. ►

HE DID NOT NOTICE ME AT ALL!

ARA ARAKANGA

You simply won't overlook this **multicolored** beauty! And yet… even though it's mostly red, the yellow and blue parts help it blend in with the surrounding foliage, blossoms, and fruit. These parrots are large, have strong wings, and can fly quickly. They use their strong claws to hold onto branches but also to capture and examine various objects–like nuts, for example, which they easily crack open with their sharp beak. ►

BRAZILIAN THREE-BANDED ARMADILLO

Even though jungles can be dangerous, this little fellow needn't worry. Its body is covered with a shell of bony slates which serve as **armor**. All the armadillo needs to do is to curl up, and it's completely free from harm! ◄

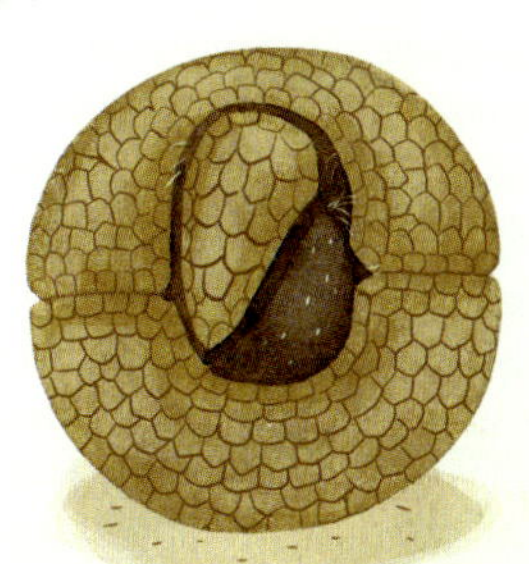

POLAR REGIONS

THE KINGDOM OF SNOW AND ICE

It's bitterly cold, plus white and icy as far as the eye can see. Floes are flowing on the icy water, and icebergs tower high above the surface. You'd be hard-pressed to find a plant anywhere around here. The locals are quite unique. Not only can they withstand living in this icy kingdom without an issue, but they can't be encountered anywhere else in the world. This is why we can consider them the kings and queens of this realm. Nobody else would dare live in polar regions.

WHERE CAN YOU FIND THE POLAR REGIONS?

Beyond the polar circle, of course! The southern region is called **Antarctica**, and the northern one **the Arctic**, just to make sure they don't get mixed up. Each pole hosts somewhat different inhabitants: for example, penguins slide on their bellies near the South Pole, while polar bears romp on floes near the North Pole. Don't forget, though: both poles are some of the least hospitable areas on the planet. ▸

HOW CAN YOU SURVIVE IN SUCH COLD?

A lack of green vegetation, **everlasting snow and ice**... that doesn't sound too idyllic, now, does it? So how do the inhabitants deal with it? In colder regions, the protrusions on many animal bodies–such as ears, a tail, or beak–are rather small in order not to become frostbitten. A lightish coloring helps the animals blend in with the snow and be better at hiding from predators –or at catching prey. ▴

DANGERS OF THE LAND OF ICE & SNOW

The climate is very cold at the poles and the ground is permanently frozen. That's why very few plants grow there. The northernmost regions are even covered with a permanent layer of ice! Animals that live there can't be encountered anywhere else in the world. Local birds and mammals are well equipped to live in such hostile conditions. ◂

COME CUDDLE UP

When a warm coat isn't enough, loyal friends come to the rescue. If many members of the same species **crowd together**, there are fewer losses of heat and everybody's nice and warm. The inside of the cluster is the warmest, which is why the young are having a regular sauna in there. ▼

HE WHO'S COVERED IS SAFE

A thick layer of fur, plumage, or subcutaneous fat is a fundamental requirement. It's safe to say that no one around is feeling guilty about eating fatty foods. The animals also have special equipment so that their limbs don't become frostbitten and no needless heat losses occur. ▼

INUITS – PEOPLE OF THE NORTH

There are people who live in the land of eternal ice. They're called Inuits. In the past, they built some houses–igloos–out of ice blocks! The igloos were constructed in a way that made sure the inhabitants would be shielded from the cold and wind. Iniuts are not only proficient builders but also hunters who sometimes use dog sleds. ▲

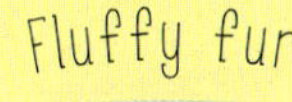

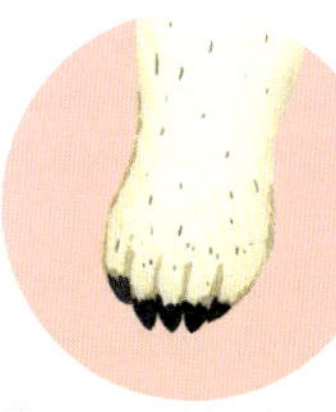

POLAR REGION INHABITANTS

TRUE WINTER SWIMMERS

EMPEROR PENGUIN

These nonflying birds, who are the only ones who spend the winter in Antarctica, have their family lives figured out: the female lays eggs and then leaves to hunt for a very long time. In the meantime, the male takes care of the eggs and carries them on its feet, covered by its brood pouch to keep them warm. In order to warm themselves up, they gather in crowds and take turns standing in the cozy circle. When the mothers return, they take the place of the fathers, who then go hunting themselves. ▸

MUSK OX

A musk ox has **doubly layered fur**. The inner layer is shorter and serves as insulation, while the outer one is longer and protects the wearer from sharp winds. Musk oxen feel most at ease when gathered in a herd: when a wolf sets its sights on them, they surround their young, close ranks, and point their sharp horns in the direction of the enemy. ◂

POLAR FOX

Polar foxes have one of the shaggiest and warmest coats of all animals. In summer, the fox is grey-brown in order to better blend in with the surrounding rocks, but it turns white in the winter, becoming indistinguishable from the snow and ice. ▾

POLAR BEAR

This majestic inhabitant of the North Pole–the Arctic–is one of the largest predators in the world. Polar bears eat very fatty foods to sustain their thick layer of subcutaneous fat that keeps them nice and warm. The animal's quite deft both in water and on dry land–the hairy paws keep it from slipping and the hollow hairs filled with air buoy it up in the water. ▴

SEAL

Just look at this cutie! Baby seals move in a very funny way. That's because their fins are still too big for them. After the young grow up, they'll become excellent swimmers and divers! Seals spend a lot of time in the water under ice where they look for food and safety from predators. They're lucky to be protected by their warm and fatty coat. ▸

Baby seal

WALRUS

This moustached creature can be often seen lying around on a floe with its pals. The tough, wrinkly skin with a thick layer of subcutaneous fat is well adapted to the cold, which is why the walrus doesn't feel chilly in the slightest. Notice also its **moustache** and **tusks**. The whiskers are as sensitive as our fingers are! Walruses use their strong tusks not only to defend themselves but also as axes when they crawl out of the water onto the floe or cut holes into ice. ▾

Cold water swimmers

ARCTIC OWL

The snow-white, subtly patterned coloring of males isn't just for decorative purposes. Its main function is making the animal blend in with the snowy surroundings. As an added bonus, the very thick plumage, along with thickly covered limbs, protects Arctic owls from the freezing cold. ▴

FORESTS

TREE KINGDOM

Forests grow all around the world, and we should value and pamper them. Not only do they produce large amounts of the oxygen we breathe, but they also host some very useful animals. When you go out for a walk in the forest, be quiet and considerate lest you needlessly disturb them. Maybe you'll be lucky and spot a squirrel, deer, or badger. Plus you can pick a basket of mushrooms, fruit, or herbs.

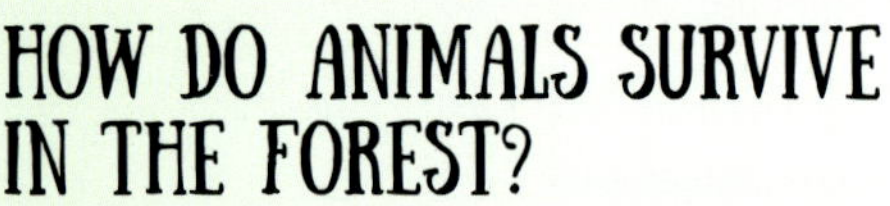

HOW DO ANIMALS SURVIVE IN THE FOREST?

They had to get used to the changing of the four seasons. Their life is generally pretty swell during spring, summer, and autumn: there's usually enough food and the temperature is nothing to worry about. The situation changes, however, once the winter arrives and forces the animals to ride out the cold months as best they can. Notice, too, that animals usually have such **coloration** that helps them blend in with their surroundings. ▸

WAIT, YOU CAN SEE ME?

WHAT'S THE WAY IT GOES IN THE FOREST?

There's a lot of green vegetation in the forest–from short grasses and small bushes to full-grown trees. Forests have no lack of moisture and food, especially in the spring and summer. Animals have to deal with **changing seasons**, over the course of which broadleaf trees shed their foliage, prepare themselves for the winter, and then regenerate once spring arrives. On the other hand, coniferous trees aren't deciduous. It's still an undeniable fact, though, that nature sleeps during the winter period. ▾

WHAT KINDS OF FORESTS ARE THERE IN THE WORLD?

Forests can be broadleaf, coniferous, or mixed–meaning that you can find both types of trees. Most forests are located in the temperate zone, which means that the weather is nicer there. If you venture farther north, you'll encounter snow forests or taigas, where the weather is slightly colder. Be it over here or over there–no matter what forest type we're talking about, you'll meet a lot of animal inhabitants in it who know the forest like the back of their paws or hooves. ◂

THIS ONE EATS & THE OTHER SLEEPS

Certain smart little devils don't like to sit around and twiddle their thumbs. Instead, they do their best to stock up for the inevitable hard times. Squirrels, for example, gather various nuts that really come in handy during the winter. Other animals go into **hibernation** in order to safely wait out the winter. All they need to do is fatten up like there's no tomorrow, find a shelter, and sleep till the spring. ▼

SEE YOU IN THE SPRING?

THERE & BACK AGAIN

And what about birds, what do they do? Before the winter starts, most insect-eating birds **leave for warmer regions** where they are warm and able to get something good to eat. Once the winter is over, they return home. Most of the birds that don't set out for warmer regions grow warmer or thicker fur or plumage. ◀

I LIKE FORESTS.

EXPERT CABIN-DWELLERS

A lot of people live in forests, but not everybody can live in as great harmony with nature as some Canadians can. Even though local lumberjacks cut trees down, some inhabit their wooden log cabins in a way that impacts the nature as little as possible. ▶

FOREST INHABITANTS

FLEXIBLE CREATURES

RED SQUIRREL

This agile little critter is well prepared for living in the forest, and especially for the hostile winter. Before winter arrives, the squirrel **gathers** nuts and saves them for hard times. In order to keep its ears warm, it "puts on" a warmer coat to wear during the winter–meaning that its fur gets longer. High up the trees, squirrels are well camouflaged in their nest. ▼

BROWN BEAR

Apart from their "fake" hibernation, bears are protected from the cold by their thick, warm fur, furry paws, and large body. Even though they fatten up and get a thick layer of subcutaneous fat, they can never be quite sure that they won't happen to get hungry while they're sleeping! ▲

WILD BOAR

This satisfied family's got it all figured out–the piglets, especially, are colored in a way that allows them to easily blend in with the surrounding growth. Wild boars have a **strong little snout** that they use to dig up roots, tubers, and insect larvae. They're omnivores and thus don't have to worry about getting food in the winter. Their fur gets darker and thicker to keep them warm in winter. ▼

WINTER SLEEPERS

Some animals, such as hedgehogs or dormice, simply **sleep** through the winter. Dormice hide, curl up, and use their tail as a cover. For other animals, however, the hibernation is fake– meaning that they wake up in the middle of winter, find something to eat, and then go back to bed. Bears or badgers do precisely that! ▲

Mid-winter snack

COMMON LYNX

This handsome fellow can be found in high-laying northern forests. Its **beautiful, thick fur** protects it from adverse weather, and additionally helps the animal camouflage itself so that it can hunt well. The lynx has wide, furry paws which function as snowshoes and prevent it from falling through the snow. Do you think that its ears are funny? You'll be surprised to know, then, that the black tufts on the top increase hearing! ▸

WOODPECKER

Let's not forget the **forest doctor**: the woodpecker! They let us know whether the forest is healthy, or not. They have great equipment to use: a strong, sharp beak which they use to chisel the wood, a swift tongue to fish out the occasional tasty morsel, a pair of climbing feet, and long tail feathers on which they lean. Woodpeckers even carve out hollows in the trees and live in them! ▾

EUROPEAN ELK

Elks can be found mainly in the forests up north. These majestic creatures boast long, slender legs that enable them to run quickly and swim excellently. The hooves consist of two toes that allow their owner to maintain balance and not sink into snowdrifts. The males can grow **large, beautiful antlers** which may frighten anybody who would be foolish enough to challenge their wearer. However, since growing them consumes a lot of energy, the elk sheds them before the winter arrives. ▴

WATER KINGDOM

LIVING UNDERWATER

Living under the sea is no piece of cake. Ocean inhabitants had to figure out how to best camouflage themselves, hide, and get food, all of which needed to be achieved without drawing the attention of some larger creature that might be on the lookout for dinner. There's quite a lively scene under the sea: shoals of fish swim about, beautiful coral reefs teem with many odd animals, and fearless predators abound. Underwater inhabitants can be found even at huge depths.

DANGERS OF THE WATER KINGDOM

The idea of living in azure waters may seem fantastic, but know that there's certainly no **dearth** of danger. Shelter can be found, but anyone who happens to find themselves in the open sea needs to come to grips with the fact that others will declare open season on them. ▼

NOT ALL WATER IS CREATED EQUAL

We'll take a journey under the surface of seas and oceans. However, there are also places all around the world with **fresh** water–for example lakes, rivers, ponds, and even glaciers. Various animals and plants occupy their own water kingdoms. And now take into account that the water in certain rivers may ultimately flow all the way down to the sea! ▲

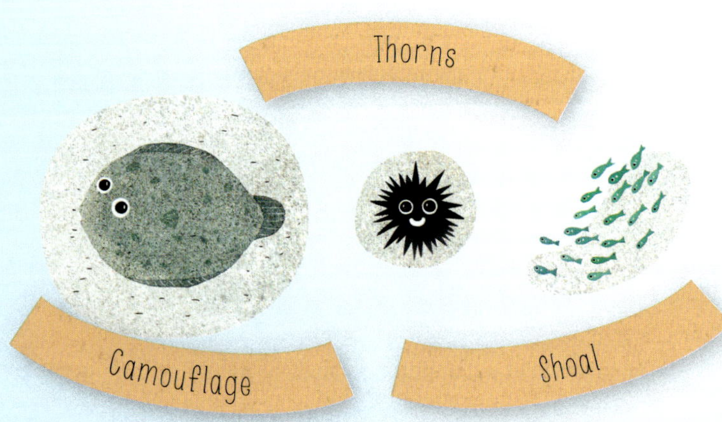

SURVIVING UNDERWATER

How to avoid all these dangers? Everybody has a different strategy: some animals camouflage themselves in order not to be spotted; others flaunt their colorful beauty. Some like to hide in a shelter, but others swim in large shoals–after all, there's superiority in numbers! And those who are the toughest of all rely on their prickly thorns or on venom to drive their enemies away. ◄

A FIN HERE, A GILL THERE

A lot of sea animals have **perfectly adapted bodies** that enable them to easily swim, hunt, and rest. Sharks, for example, possess excellent senses, and thus are great hunters. Others can hide in the sand where nobody notices them. And the deep-sea fish? These odd little monsters are able to hunt even if it's pitch black, and they can deal with extreme temperatures or pressure. ▼

PEOPLE OF THE SEAS

Many people who live on islands surrounded by water feel quite at home in it. The Thai Moken, for example, certainly know their way around: they go out to sea in fishing boats to catch fish. They know where to go to find fish and are skillful hunters. These fishers can often see well even in deep waters! ▼

LIVING UNDERWATER

Sea animals employ various **tricks** in order to make their life underwater comfortable. Some maintain a constant body temperature and can stay in warm or cold waters without seeming to mind. Most underwater animals don't drink the water but acquire it in another way. And of course, they know how to communicate with one another even though they're submerged in water! ▲

WATER INHABITANTS

ALWAYS ON THEIR GUARD

GREEN SEA TURTLE

Their front flippers serve as **paddles** and turn swimming into a walk in the park! Green sea turtles are great divers. These animals get their drinking water either from food or by consuming saltwater and then excreting the excess salt in the form of tears. When turtles decide to lay eggs, they have to crawl out of the sea onto a beach. They're slow and vulnerable on dry land, which is why they immediately flee back to the sea once the eggs are laid and buried. Turtles know that their young will infallibly head for the see waves as soon as they hatch. ▸

CAMOUFLAGED SCORPION FISH

This little predatory fish can be seen mostly at the bottom of the sea, where it patiently waits all day, perfectly disguised. It goes hunting once the night falls. Apart from the excellent camouflage, which helps it blend in with the surrounding coral reefs, the fish also relies on its speed, large mouth, and the element of surprise. ▸

SHARK – A GREAT HUNTER

Sharks have simply **incredible senses**. Their fantastic sense of smell allows them to take a whiff of a single drop of blood at huge distances! Their body, too, is well adapted, not only in shape, but also where "equipment" is concerned: the skin and shape of their fins permit easier and faster swimming, while the lateral line helps detect movement, undulation, or vibrations, and thus increases the animal's hearing. ▴

Blue whale

BLUE WHALE & PLANKTON

Blue whales are the **largest animals** to ever inhabit Earth. What's their life like? They cruise the oceans undisturbed, not having to worry about anyone else. It's quite remarkable that they feed on the little fellows known as plankton: the animal simply fills its mouth with water, strains it, and then swallows the remaining fish stew, which is full of plankton. ◂

DOLPHIN

Dolphins are truly **smart sea inhabitants**. They're smartly colored: when observed from above, their dark back blends in with the dark depths, and when viewed from down below, their light belly resembles the light ocean surface. Dolphins use their fins as rudders or brakes. They are also great jumpers! Their forehead has a bulging protrusion which sends out waves or receives them. This helps the animal to find out where things are and to communicate with other dolphins. ◂

Like a flatfish

Its normal self

Like a sea snake

MASTER OF DISGUISE

Is it a flatfish? Or a sea snake? Wait a minute; it's the good old **octopus**! Meet the mimic octopus, dear reader. It can imitate other animals in order to distract the attention of its enemies. And if even that doesn't help, the animal can always run away! ◂

ANGLERFISH

When we dive deep–someplace where sunlight can't reach, an eternal darkness reigns, and huge pressure exists–we encounter some really **strange creatures**. Let's take this anglerfish, for example: it's equipped with a large mouth with big teeth whose grasp allows no prey to escape. The main thing, however, is that the fish lures its prey by employing a glowing protrusion which resembles a lamp or little fishing rod. ▸

Anglerfish luring its prey

GRASS REGIONS

GRASS HERE, BUSHES THERE

We're in an African savanna, one of the best-known grass regions in the world. Similar ones can be found in America, Asia, and Australia. What do they have in common? All of them involve a dry climate, sharp sunlight, grass, bushes, even a couple of trees here and there. And mainly, the locals are very resilient. Not only can they deal with the changing of dry and rainy seasons, but also with the fact that they're constantly pursued by something bent on eating them.

STEPPES OR SAVANNAS?

Grass regions are called many names–it depends on their location. What can be said with certainty, though, is that it doesn't really matter whether we call it "a steppe" or "a savanna"–it looks pretty much the same. It's not a desert, nor a forest, but rather something in between. Rain is pretty rare in grass regions, which is why mostly resilient grasses, shrubs, and in places even a tree or two grow there. ◂

DANGERS OF SAVANNAS

There are two seasons in savannas, not four: **drought** and **the rains**. During the dry season, it rains either very little, or not at all, meaning that animals and plants have to find a way to do without water. Wildfires can even break out! However, once the rainy season arrives and more than enough moisture falls, everything starts growing like crazy. On the downside, lower-laying regions may experience floods. ▾

Dry season

Rainy season

SURVIVING IN SAVANNAS

Fast legs are the basic requirement for living in the savanna, where predators with huge appetites abound. Some animals resort to **camouflaging** themselves in order to be at least somewhat able to hide out in the open. You see, playing hide-and-seek in tall grass is simply the bee's knees! Those who have a long neck or thick skin should really congratulate themselves on their luck. ▴

DROUGHT OR RAIN, WE DON'T CARE

Some animals and plants can make do with very little when water is concerned. For example, certain plants have really long roots that they use to reach underground water. Others contain **water reservoirs** inside their body. This gives them access to all the liquid necessary, This goes for animals too! Many animals travel long distances to get water. ▼

Warning

I CAN SEE AROUND THE CORNER

Savannas bustle with activity. There are almost always some zebras, antelopes, or other ungulates that graze on grass. However, they always need to be on their toes. They often have special partners to help them achieve this. For example, monkeys or ostriches may let them know if any danger appears on the horizon. The problem is that the surrounding tall grass may be hiding a lion, cheetah, or another predator who's always poised to attack. ◄

HUNTER-GATHERERS

African savannas still are home to tribes that make a living either by gathering (honey, among other things) or by hunting (normally using the bow and arrow). They've been living this traditional lifestyle for a long time, and thus know very well how to get around in the savanna. As modern times arrived, however, many such tribes slowly disappeared and took their traditions and customs with them. ►

Local tribe members

GRASSLAND INHABITANTS

TOUGH GUYS

ZEBRA

The coat of this **striped beauty** plays an important part in the animal's self-defense. When zebras are gathered in a herd, it's more difficult for lions and leopards to tell them apart, although each zebra has a unique pattern! Zebras have great eyesight and hearing and can run pretty fast. They possess strong teeth, and therefore don't mind grazing on grass. If water is scarce, they travel anywhere they can find it. ▸

ELEPHANT

An elephant's large ears function as fans and cool their owner down. Their trunk is strong and nimble– an elephant can lift many things and also suck in water with it! Their wrinkly skin is good when one needs to cool off, and after the animal decides to roll around in the mud for a bit, neither insects nor sun bother it anymore. Elephants don't allow anything to happen to their herd; the cow elephant in charge even remembers where to find water, food, or safe shelter. Plus they're so big that nobody dares challenge them! ▴

GIRAFFE

These beanpoles have one serious advantage: due to their **huge neck**, they can reach all the way up to the treetops, poke the juiciest leaves out with their tongue, and get water out of them. Unlike other animals, a giraffe doesn't have to chew on dry grass. The camouflage also helps with blending in among the surrounding leaves and shadows. If these animals are gathered in a herd, no lion dares attack them. And as if that wasn't enough, they're always on their guard. A giraffe needs only 5 to 30 minutes of sleep a day. ▸

LION

These majestic hunters mostly like to spend their days resting in the shade. They go hunting only when the night falls and it gets colder. Hunting is usually the responsibility of lionesses because they are swifter and faster than lions. Lions greatly value their pack– not only do they hunt together, they also socialize in packs. The **fearless lion** guards its family jealously and roars like mad whenever an uninvited guest arrives. ◂

TERMITES

Their nests are full of labyrinthine chambers, among them kitchens, farms, pantries, or children's rooms – everything's at hand! This complicated network of tunnels also serves as a ventilation system, keeping a constant temperature in the nest. Other savanna inhabitants also find the nests useful as watchtowers, steps, or food supplies. All the same, termites are a subject of secret envy. ▸

HELLO! CAN YOU HEAR ME UP THERE?

BIRDS THAT AREN'T AFRAID OF FIRE

Are you wondering why birds hang around **wildfires**? Why they don't flee like any other animal does? Many African bird species circle the fires because there's dinner to be found in there. The birds simply gobble up the beetles that escape from the fire. ▾

ANT BEARS

It looks like a pig, has ears like a rabbit, and gulps down ants like an anteater would. Meet the ant bear! During the day, it sleeps in its den where the sun can't reach it, coming out only at night. Once outside, an ant bear employs its strong legs to dig up ants and termites, catching them with its **long, sticky tongue**. These animals are great diggers, and when there's any danger lurking about, they dig up a hole and hide in it in a flash! ▴

Published in 2022 by Windmill Books,
an Imprint of Rosen Publishing
29 East 21st Street, New York, NY 10010

Author: Pavla Hanáčková
Illustrator: Linh Dao

Cataloging-in-Publication Data

Names: Dao, Linh. | Hanáčková, Pavla.
Title: Why penguins don't get cold / by Linh Dao and Pavla Hanáčková.
Description: New York : Windmill Books, 2022. | Series: Amazing nature
Identifiers: ISBN 9781499487626 (pbk.) | ISBN 9781499487640 (library bound) | ISBN 9781499487633 (6 pack) | ISBN 9781499487657 (ebook)
Subjects: LCSH: Adaptation (Biology)--Juvenile literature. | Adaptation (Physiology)--Juvenile literature. | Animal behavior--Juvenile literature.
Classification: LCC QH546.H363 2022 | DDC 591.4--dc23

Printed in the United States of America

CPSIA Compliance Information: Batch BSWM22: For Further Information contact Rosen Publishing, New York, New York at 1-800-237-9932